RE-ENGINEERING CUSTOMER SERVICE

RE-ENGINEERING CUSTOMER SERVICE

A Key to Quality Customer Service,
Relationship to Business Operations, Strategy,
and Information Technology

Dr. Bob L Ssekyanzi, PhD.

Copyright © 2024 by Dr. Bob L Ssekyanzi, PhD.

ISBN:	Softcover	979-8-3694-3383-6
	eBook	979-8-3694-3373-7

All rights reserved. No part of this book may be reproduced or transmitted in any form or by any means, electronic or mechanical, including photocopying, recording, or by any information storage and retrieval system, without permission in writing from the copyright owner.

Any people depicted in stock imagery provided by Getty Images are models, and such images are being used for illustrative purposes only.
Certain stock imagery © Getty Images.

Print information available on the last page.

Rev. date: 11/07/2024

To order additional copies of this book, contact:
Xlibris
844-714-8691
www.Xlibris.com
Orders@Xlibris.com
863886

CONTENTS

Introduction vii
The world of service is changing 1
References 83
Dedication 87
About the Author 89

INTRODUCTION

Reengineering is a radically new process of organizational change that many companies are using to renew their commitment to customer service. By focusing on making improvements in all dimensions of the service organization—the human dimension, the work process dimension, and the technological dimension—reengineering helps companies overcome the systemic work barriers that interfere with efforts to achieve higher levels of customer satisfaction and product offering. Though reengineering is a long, and sometimes a difficult process that requires strong leadership, extensive participation, and a three-phased approach, it often results in dramatic improvements in how an organization responds to customer needs and expectations.

As businesses in all categories try to keep pace with the competitive environment in the global marketplace, the challenges of meeting customer expectations have become increasingly more demanding. In all accounts, customers have a shortage of time, with plenty of choices. The stakes are high to win and retain customers, as well as ensure customers speak enthusiastically to others about the value received from their relationship with a particular business establishment for a particular product or service. As it turns out, succeeding in the marketplace and remain competitive, requires listening to the voices of your customers throughout the entire journey of that relationship. This is the essence of understanding the customer experience. Good customer experience is built by giving structure to all of the customer interaction points according to organizational culture or need for digitization or any such components. Aligning various customer-facing processes to create an enhanced customer experience might end up consuming a significant amount of dedicated time and effort from an organization's management as well as other employees; hence the need for reengineering the concept of customer service.

By all accounts, the quality of customer service is the key differentiator between good, bad and indifferent companies. Good quality customer service keeps customers coming back; bad customer service drives customers away, taking their friends, family and workmates with them. All else being equal, good quality customer service gives companies the edge over their competitors. Customer satisfaction is defined as a measurement that determines how happy customers are with a company's products, services, and capabilities to meet their needs. Customer satisfaction information, including surveys and ratings, can help a company determine how to best improve or changes its products and services. An organization's main focus must be to satisfy its customers. This applies to industrial firms, retail and wholesale businesses, government bodies, service companies, nonprofit organizations, and every subgroup within an organization.

Successful reengineering projects in diverse industries and locations demonstrate how companies can expand the dimensions of their reengineering projects. Customer service is one of the important key elements to maintaining good customer relations and growing a successful business. Effective and quality customer service allows a company to stay connected with its customers and to receive valuable feedback. Without the connection between the company and the customers, most businesses fail to remain viable. It is very important to note that all else being equal; a company's good and quality customer service provides the edge over its competitors.

Customer service is the ability of an organization to supply their customers' wants and needs at a level that meets or exceeds their expectations. Customers come in different shapes, fashions, live in completely a different world, and overall, speak a different language. No matter the main objective of the company, the customers expect to be taken care of in such a way that their needs are met to the best possible way from their point of view. As far as managing customers is concerned, an important non-product benefit which affects customers' feelings, attitudes, intentions and beliefs about the company can be analyzed based on the activities used by the company to support the consumers' experience with the company's products/services. It follows, therefore, that good customer service is the lifeblood of any business. Thus, to have good customer service, it is unquestionably essential that customers are satisfied with the products and/or services being offered to meet their needs.

As I think of the concept of customer service, the challenge all businesses are facing is how to move from today's rigid, procedure-based customer service structure to tomorrow's dynamic, process-based and service-driven culture. In my opinion, given the constant changes in the global marketplace, the key is focused reengineering. It is very important to note that most of the business world has heard of the term "reengineering." It is a common jargon in industry and all over the business environment today and comes in a number of shapes and colors. Reengineering (Davenport, Thomas, H. 1993) is viewed by its creators as, "the fundamental rethinking and radical redesign of business processes to achieve dramatic improvements in critical, contemporary measures of performance such as cost, quality, service and speed."

Customer service is based on the concept of the services provided to customers before, during and after purchasing and using goods and/or services. Good and/or quality customer service entails an experience that meets or exceeds customers' expectations. Good customer service produces satisfied customers. Bad customer service can generate complaints and as a consequence, can result in lost sales and business stagnation because consumers might take their business to a competitor.

The concept of customer service is based on a 4 (four) stage model which shows how the organization can achieve growth by capturing and retaining customers. The customer service concept model can be used to determine where an organization stands as far as serving its segment of customers are concerned. It is essential to note that customer service is made up of people; their capabilities, competencies, attitudes, engagement, continuity and strategy, the organizational processes; the creativity and consistency embedded in carrying out the business and finally the organizational culture; the credibility and commitment to customer service from throughout the organization. Delivering a high standard of customer service can help to increase customer numbers through repeat business and referrals. Likewise, a poor customer experience can have greater impact on an organization's reputation and potential future business operations.

No matter how proactive you are, you'll never be able to get in front of every customer issue. To make sure you learn about the good, the bad, and the ugly experience your customers have, create an easily accessible way for customers to give feedback. Whether it's a phone survey at the end of a service call, an email survey sent directly from your CRM tool, or a form on the "Contact Us" page of your website, creating a means for customers to give feedback makes it easier for you to learn what needs improvement. It also helps keep unhappy customers from voicing their displeasure on highly visible places like your social media pages.

There are a few pitfalls that can trap a reengineering effort and process redesign phase of which one must be aware. One pitfall of classic reengineering techniques is that they may lead a company to become overly focused on financial returns. The philosophy should be to foster a balanced approach between cost reduction goals and improved customer service. By doing so, buying-in from all stakeholders is encouraged and facilitated. Note that reengineering the customer service function first has a hidden benefit in that it enables the organization to "lead by example," and actually becomes the role model for a well-timed, strategically paced reengineering of other organizations in the company, in a manner that allows the company to avoid the culture shock that plagues many whole-company projects.

All things considered; it is very essential to note (Champ, James 1995) that customers have become more powerful than they used to be. They are now empowered through social conversation. The geographical barriers are, to most extent, gone for good. With the changing global marketplace landscape, companies to be successful, many brands need to think customer service re-engineering as the new order to meet the challenges of today's business environment. Customer service re-engineering requires a new mindset as against the old system of rendering service. It requires organizations to embrace the concept of critical thinking and situation analysis.

THE WORLD OF SERVICE IS CHANGING

Over the past few years we have witnessed significant changes in business and the economy which have impacted on the way organizations and customers relate to service. One of the main changes is the move from a transactional economy to a relationship economy – which has altered how customer service is viewed in relation to business performance. It is becoming more and more evident that today's customers are savvy, discerning and demanding. They expect organizations to relate to them as individuals, not just as transactions and this is affecting the whole value chain. Customer service expectations are part of interactions with customers, suppliers, partners and internal customers with the quality of an organization's relationships becoming a determining factor in their success. So, if satisfying customers is becoming more difficult and the links with business performance more evident how can you make sure your customer service has a positive impact?

A strategic commitment to customer service

Customer service is recognized and articulated as a central organizational objective. There must be senior-level accountability for customer service, and the individuals' job descriptions should include clearly defined customer service objectives. Appropriate measures must be in place to assess the impact of key stages of the customer experience as experienced by customers on a daily basis; and as such, there must be appropriate customer service experience and expertise in the company's boardroom.

Customer insight

Organizations have systematic methods for gathering customer feedback and act on the results. Organizations have a deep understanding of the profile, priorities and needs of the customers they serve and use this to reform standards of customer service

Time and time again, customer service takes place while performing a transaction for the customer, such as making a sale or returning an item. Customer service can take the form of an in-person interaction, a phone call, self-service systems, or by various other means. Good customer service is partly defined by the industry, but a large part of how your company defines it will determine what good customer service means to you and your customer segment.

Every human being in this world is, in one way or another, affected by the concept of services on a daily basis: Communication services, food services, transportation services, entertainment services, and other intangible services, to name a few. With regard to the economy, it is safe to say that no economy can effectively function without the infrastructure based on the concept of quality customer services.

Customer service is an extremely important part of maintaining ongoing client relationships, which are keys to continuing revenue. For this reason, many companies have worked hard to increase their customer satisfaction levels. Although many people may work behind the scenes at a company, it is primarily the personnel that interact directly with customers that form customers' perceptions of the company as a whole.

It is very important to point out that customer service begins long before the first sign of trouble and the crisis begins. Customer service isn't an after-sell thought. And it is separate from technical support. Fixing problems and responding to troubled customers whose need for assistance is covered by a warranty or service contract isn't customer support, it's an obligation. Customer service is listening to your customers and truly understanding their needs, wants, and desires — helping them achieve their objectives and a memorable shopping experience. It's not about giving things away for free; it is simply about caring and acting sincerely in the customers' interests, not yours.

Excellent customer service is demonstrated when solutions are offered before they're asked for, when introductions are made to advance an idea or create a new opportunity, and when potential problems are discussed before they have an opportunity to develop. Take the first step in delivering outstanding customer service: talk to your best customers, discuss their business objectives and goals, focus on their interest, and explore how you and your company can advance their activity. Don't focus on your products or services, don't worry about your quota, and don't pitch your offering. Just care. And you'll be rewarded with repeat business and referrals beyond your imagination.

Good or bad, customer service leaves an indelible impression on potential and existing customers, even in today's fast paced, technological environment. And truth be told, most folks will endure more, pay more, and show fierce loyalty for courteous treatment, small perks, and the feeling of being valued. Whether it's a liberal "return policy" at a store, businesses that acknowledge and reward your "relationship anniversary" with them, or service with a smile go a long way in attracting a certain segment of customers. Good customer service translates into repeat business, an increased bottom line, and the company's economic survival. And that just makes good business sense even on bad days!

Providing good customer service enables a company to create a distinctive position for itself in relation to competitors. This requires investment in employees, training and processes to maintain high standards. However there is a payback: good customer service can reduce marketing costs and some other operational costs. Additionally, providing good customer service also means that customers have fewer complaints about the quality of the products and/or services they receive from your company. Dealing with complaints can be costly. So, again, by providing good customer service, the companies reduce the time and costs of resolving customer-related issues, and invest more in innovative ideas which can add value to the company's overall operation.

With the ability to quickly adapt and handle customer concerns, the concept of customer service represents an area businesses excel in. Good customer service has the potential to alter consumer viewpoints and provide businesses with important feedback related to the products and services being offered.

Providing services "with a smile" used to be quite enough to please consumers. Today, however, the majority of businesses strive to differentiate themselves in the marketplace by offering a "service guarantee." Unlike a product warranty, which promises to repair or replace the faulty product, service guarantees typically offer the unhappy customers with a refund, discount, or free services.

Service quality is a very challenging subject, as shown by the need for a definition that includes five essential dimensions: responsiveness; reliability; assurance; empathy; and tangibles.

These five dimensions are used in order to introduce the concept of effective customer service quality gap that pose a great challenge to companies as they try to reconcile the differences between customers' expectations of the services and the perceptions of the actual services rendered.

Quality customer service begins with the design of the service delivery system applied by the company. Thus, concepts borrowed from product design such as Taguchi methods, poka-yoke, and quality function deployment are applied to the design of service systems.

It is very essential to note that the assessment of quality customer service is made during the service delivery process. Each customer contact is referred to as a moment of truth, an opportunity to satisfy or dissatisfy the customer. Customer satisfaction with a service can be defined by comparing perceptions of service received with expectations of service desired. When customer expectations are exceeded, service is perceived to of exceptional quality-and also to be a pleasant surprise. When expectations are not met, however, service quality is deemed unacceptable. When expectations are confirmed by perceived service, quality is satisfactory.

In order to fully understand how the concept of customer service works, it is very important to look at the following **"4 (four) Cs"** of Customer Service:

The 4 Cs of Customer Service

When I think of the effort by any business undertaking to attract customers, there are four words which come to my mind, and in light of the companies striving to offer their consumers; I call these four words the **4 Cs** of customer service- **Consistency,**

Communication, Commitment, and Completeness. In light of the 4 Cs, the following is a detailed explanation of what they entail and how important they are to the concept of quality customer service:

Consistency: Consistency means that the company's customers will always receive the same level service during each time they come to the establishment. It follows, therefore, that no matter how many branches your company has, customers receive positive experience. When companies provide consistent customer service experience, a word-of-mouth quickly spreads to new customers as a result of the company's ability to be consistent in its product/service offerings.

Communication: The second C in the process of providing customer service means that the company' employees are kept posted of the developments pertaining to how customers' needs are met. This C means that employees are given the means to communicate the customers' perception of the organization to the leaders. It means that customers are able to initiate communication with the company regarding their personal experience with the products or services being offered by the company. Innovative and free channels of communication must be created in order for customers and the company to find new ways of improving service and products.

Commitment: In order for the company to provide great service, there must be an element of commitment from the company's leadership. Commitment must be visible through action. Company leaders should commit to finding ways and means of determining what is important to the company's customer. Company leaders should develop and adhere to the core values for the company. Company leaders should regularly communicate their commitment with the entire members of the company. Company's commitment must be based on long-term implementation, and as such, commitment requires continuous evaluation whereby associates and prospective customer can provide feedback on what needs to be improved and/or eliminated.

Completeness: Completeness means ensuring that what matters to the customers is identified and utilized in developing the company's services and/or product concept. It is very essential to note, therefore, that completeness means identifying one's internal customers in order to determine how to meet their needs as well. Once the commitment is in place, the need to ensure that everyone within the company is on the same page is very important to the company's success. All areas of the company's operations must be aware of how their everyday activities impact both internal as well as external customers. Completely commit to providing great customer service if your company is to effectively compete in the global marketplace!

As the competition in the global marketplace continues to pose a challenge to organizations, provision of customer service must be a focal point for companies in order to ensure that consumers understand how important they are to respective companies. Companies must strive to make sure that customers are able to see, hear and feel what they mean to the organizations by establishing **Consistency** during all customer interactions, followed by application of effective **Communication** of process, products, and policy changes. **Commitment** of provision of quality products, customer service and followed by the element of **Completeness** of the company's purpose of existence.

Nature of the Service Sector

To understand the importance of customer service and its implications in the operations of any given organization, it is very essential to understand the nature of service. The distinction between products and services is somehow difficult to make, because the purchase of products is accompanied by some facilitating services and the purchase of services more than often includes facilitating goods. But at the end is the consumer who has the final voice in the purchasing process.

A service is an activity or series of activities of more or less intangible nature that usually, but not necessarily, take place in interactions between customer and service associates and/or systems of the service provider, which are provided as solutions to customer problems or needs.

Services can be classified in terms of two dimensions: **The degree of labor intensity**, which is between labor costs and capital cost; and **the degree of customer interaction and customization**, which is between the customer's ability to affect personally the nature of the services/products delivered.

For many people, service is synonymous with servitude and brings to mind workers flipping hamburgers and waiting on tables. However, the service sector that has grown significantly over the past 7 decades cannot be accurately described as composed only of low-wage or low-skilled jobs in department stores and fast-food restaurants. Instead, as **Table 1.1** shows, employment in 2004 was divided among a number of high-skilled categories such as professional and business services, health care and social assistance, and educational services.

Today, service industries are the source of economic leadership. During the past 50 years, more than 54 million new jobs have been created in the service sector to absorb the influx of women into the workforce and provide an alternative to the lack of job opportunities in the manufacturing sector. The service industries now account for approximately 80 percent of the national income in the United States. Given that there is a limit to how many cars a consumer can use and how much one can eat and drink, this should not be surprising at all. The appetite for services, however, especially innovative ones, is insatiable. The nature of customer service in global marketplace has moved past the mere transactional nature of service provision to one of quality experience-based relationships.

Table 1.1: Distribution of U.S. Employment by Industry Segments

Distribution of U.S. Employment by Industry, 2004.			
Information	2%		
Transportation & Utilities	4%		
Other Services	5%		
State, and Local government, except education & Hospitals	23% 6%		
Financial Activities	6%		
Leisure & Hospitality	9%		
Educational Services	10%		
Healthcare and social Assistance	11%		
Professional & Business Services	12%		
Retail & Whole Trade	16%		
Natural Resources & Mining	1%		
Construction	5%		
Manufacturing	11%		
Federal Government	2%		

Dr. Bob L Ssekyanzi, PhD.

Creating Value to Customers

It is very essential to note that creating value in service requires organizations to think of customers as individuals. It is also imperative that organizations provide the best services possible. It is also very essential for the organizations to know who the customers are and identify potential and current customers. Long term relationship and customer satisfaction are created through the customization and contact that the customers receive from the service provider. Because services are a combination of knowledge-related, they are consumed and the customers are often participants in the process, and as such, there is an opportunity to tailor the services to the needs of the customers and to create new value to the service provided. The essence of quality customer service is vested in forming a relationship with customers- a relationship that customers feel is sustainable and beneficial to both sides.

To provide good and quality customer service, companies must ensure that consistently their customer service process has the following:

- Become familiar with the customers
- Know customers' expectations
- Tell customers what to expect and eliminate surprises
- Maintain consistency
- Live up to customers' expectations
- Communicate with customers through the method easier for customers to use.

It is very important to note that it is much harder to regain credibility that to keep it. To cultivate credibility it is essential to bear in mind the following elements:

- Practice consistency service provision
- Keep promises to your customers
- Develop expertise in serving your customers
- Become a team in providing quality service
- Show dedication to your customers
- Treat every customer with the same level of respect
- Apologize whenever there is a mishap in the process of rendering services.

Having credibility is an important element of the reputation of the organization. Companies exceed customer expectations by focusing improvement efforts in three essential areas: customer friendly processes; associates' commitment to customer service; and customer dialog. In order to compete effectively in the global marketplace, companies must be excellent in all three areas mentioned above in order to achieve excellent customer service. The first step in improving customer service is the assessment of each of the critical aspects of the focus areas identified above. The assessment acts as a strategic customer service improvement plan and training needs analysis that leads to accomplishment of the customer service objectives.

Customer Satisfaction

Customer satisfaction became a popular topic in marketing during the 1980s and is one of the most debated topics in the global business marketplace. Most discussions on customer satisfaction involve customer expectation of the service delivery, actual delivery of the customer experience, and expectations that aim at either unmet expectations or exceeded. If expectations are exceeded, positive disconfirmation results, while on the flip side, a negative disconfirmation results when customers' experience is poorer than expected. In today's world of constant changes and intense competition in the global marketplace, the key to sustainable competitive advantage is based on delivering high quality customer services which engender satisfied customers.

Exceed Expectations

Not all returns can be exchanged. Many customers will only want their money back. That's okay. After you've exhausted the above selling opportunities and you've satisfied the customer, the chances are good that he or she will return to shop with you another day. So, if all else fails, give them a refund with a genuine smile. And thank them for their time and patronage. In my stores, we made the return as much fun as the sale. We wanted the last thought the customer had of us to be "I want to come back again" - which, after all, is the same thought we want them to think when they buy.

Remember, an exchange is better than no sale, but a satisfied customer is more important than a return policy. Never let your employees be about "the policy." Encourage them to be about serving the customer experience. Customers today do not want their expectations met (satisfied) they want them exceeded **(See Figure: 1.1)**

Engaging customers and welcoming them demonstrates that the company values them and cares about their needs.
Figure: 1.1

Re-engineering Customer Service

Customer satisfaction is at the heart of the selling process. One estimate is that it costs five times as much to attract new customers as it does to keep an existing one. The relationship between the customer and the organization is, therefore, an important one. Building customer relationships can be seen as moving up a ladder. At the top rung of the ladder are your loyal customers (advocates). The ladder consists of four main rungs (with 4 being the highest):

- 4 – Advocates
- 3 - Regular customers
- 2 - Occasional users
- 1 - One-off purchasers

The extent to which customers move up the ladder depends on how well they are treated by the organization. Well focused sales methods and attention to individual detail is likely to encourage customers to move up the ladder.

Customer satisfaction is a marketing term that measures how products or services supplied by a company meet or surpass a customer's expectation. Customer satisfaction is important because it provides marketers and business owners with a metric that they can use to manage and improve their business operations. In a survey of nearly 200 senior marketing managers, 71 percent responded that they found a customer satisfaction metric very useful in managing and monitoring their businesses.

When should you consider BPR

The problem with BPR is that the larger you are, the more expensive it is to implement. A startup, five months after launch, might undergo a pivot including business process reengineering that only has minimal costs to execute.

However, once an organization grows, it will have a harder and more expensive time to completely reengineer its processes. But they are also the ones who are forced to change due to competition and unexpected marketplace shifts.

But more than being industry-specific, the call for BPR is always based on what an organization is aiming for. BPR is effective when companies need to break the mold and turn the tables in order to accomplish ambitious goals. For such measures, adopting any other process management options will only be rearranging the deck chairs on the Titanic.

Here are the top six reasons why customer satisfaction is one of the most important aspect of any given business operation:

(a) Customer satisfaction is a leading indicator of consumer repurchases intentions and loyalty.

Customer satisfaction provides the best indicator of how likely consumers will buy the company's services and/or products. Asking customers to rate their satisfaction of the services they get from the company on a scale of 1-10 is a good way to gauge whether they will become repeat customers or advocates. If customers give your company a rating of 7 and above, this can be considered satisfied, and as such, the company can safely expect those customers to come back and make repeat purchases. Customers who give your company a rating of 9 or 10 are your potential advocates whom you can leverage to become evangelists for your company.

Scores of 6 and below are warning signs that some of your customers are unhappy and at risk of leaving you for your competitors. When that happens, these customers must be put on a watch list and followed up so that determination can be made as to why they are not satisfied, and make every effort to meet their expectations.

(b) Customer Satisfaction is a point differentiation.

In a competitive global marketplace where all businesses compete for almost the same segments of customers, customer satisfaction is one of the key differentiator. Companies that succeed in these cut-throat environments are the ones that make customer satisfaction a key element of their day-to-day business operation strategy. It is very essential to note that companies that offer amazing customer experience create environments where satisfaction is extremely his and customer advocates are plenty.

(c) Customer Satisfaction is based on the concept of reducing customer churn

According to the Accenture global customer satisfaction report (2008), price is not the main reason for customer churn; it is actually poor customer service that stands out as the main reason for customer churn. Customer satisfaction is the metric you can use to reduce customer churn. By measuring and tracking customer satisfaction companies can put new processes in place that can increase the overall quality of customer service. It is generally recommended that this process be evaluated every six months in order to measure its effectiveness.

(d) Customer Satisfaction Increases the lifetime value of customers

Satisfaction plays an important role in how much revenue a customer generates for a company. In a study by InfoQuest, it was found that a totally satisfied customer contributes 2.7 times more revenue than a somewhat satisfied customer. Additionally, a totally satisfied customer contributes 16 times more revenue than a somewhat dissatisfied customer. Successful companies understand the importance of customer lifetime value. If a company can increase customer lifetime value, it increases the returns on its marketing dollar. It is very essential to note that customer lifetime value is a beneficiary of high customer satisfaction and good customer retention.

(e) Customer Satisfaction reduces negative word of mouth

Customer satisfaction is tightly linked to revenue and repeat purchases. What often gets forgotten is how customer satisfaction negatively impacts the company's overall business operations. It is one thing to lose customers because they were unhappy. On the contrary, it is another thing to completely lose 30 or 40 customers because of some bad word of mouth. In order for companies to either avoid or eliminate the bad word of mouth, an effective process that focuses on measuring the level of customer satisfaction on an ongoing basis must be instituted and monitored constantly. By continuously tracking changes in customer satisfaction, companies will be able to keep up with trends and identify if customers are actually happy with the products and services being offered. According to McKinsey, an unhappy customer tells between 10-20 people about their experience. In fact, 15% of unhappy customers tell over 30 people about their experience at a particular store.

(f) With the concept of Customer Satisfaction, it is cheaper to retain customers than acquire new ones

It is without a doubt that customers cost money to acquire. It costs seven to eight times more to acquire new customers that it does to retain the existing customers. If that stat does not strike accord with your company, then there is not more that can be done to demonstrate why customer satisfaction is one of the important aspects of business operations.

Customer satisfaction is influenced by customers' perceptions of quality (Zeithaml and Bitner, 2000). Customer service quality is an antecedent of the broader concept of customer satisfaction (Lee et al., 2000) and the relationship between service quality and loyalty is mediated by satisfaction (Fullerton and Taylor, 2002).

Dimensions of Quality Service

In any organization, services are very difficult for customers to evaluate before the fact. Since services are intangible and consumed simultaneously with production, companies are presented with the challenge of measuring and achieving quality customer service. The following are dimensions of quality customer service that companies should strive to implement in their customer service procedures:

Responsiveness

The dimension of responsiveness focuses on the willingness to help customers and to provide prompt service. Keeping customers waiting, particularly for no apparent reason, creates unnecessary negative perception of quality customer service. In the event a customer service occurs, the ability to recover quickly and with exceptional professionalism can create very positive perceptions of quality service. For example, serving complimentary drinks on a delayed flight can turn a potentially poor customer experience into one that is remembered positively.

Reliability

The reliability dimension of customer service deals with the ability to perform the promised service both dependably and accurately. Reliable service performance is a customer expectation and means that the service rendered is accomplished on time, in the same manner, and without errors time and time again. For example, opening the grocery store at approximately the same time everyday is very important to most people. Reliability also extends into the back office, where accuracy in billing and record keeping is part and partial of the expectation.

Assurance

The assurance dimension of customer service focuses on the knowledge and courtesy of company associates as well as their ability to convey trust and confidence. This dimension of customer service includes the following features: competence to perform the needed services; politeness and respect for the customers; effective communication with the customers; and last *but not least, the general attitude that the server has customer's best interest at heart.*

Empathy

The empathy dimension of customer service aims at providing care and individualized customer attention. Empathy includes the following features: approachability; sensitivity; and effort to understand the customer's needs. One example of empathy is the ability of an airline gate attendant to make a customer's missed connection the attendant's own problem and to find a quick resolution.

Tangibles

The tangibles dimension of customer service focuses on the physical facilities, equipments, personnel, and communication materials. The condition of the physical surroundings (e.g., cleanliness,) is tangible evidence of the care and attention to detail that are exhibited by the service provider. This dimension also can extend to the conduct of other customers in the service (e.g., a noisy guest in the next room a hotel).

Customers use the above five mentioned dimensions to formulate their judgments of the quality of the services, which are based on a comparison between expected and perceived services. The gap between expected and perceived services is a measure of customer service quality; satisfaction is either negative or positive.

Measuring Customer Service Quality

Measuring service quality is a great challenge to companies because customer satisfaction is determined by many various intangible factors. Unlike products with physical features that can be objectively measured (e.g., the fit and finish of a car), customer service quality contains many psychological features (e.g., the ambiance of a restaurant). Additionally, customer service quality often extends beyond the immediate encounter because, as in the case of health care, it has an impact on a person's future quality of life.

Customer Quality Service by Design

Customer quality service can neither be inspected into the service/products offered, nor somehow added on, and this same observation applies to the concept of services. A concern for quality service or product begins with the design of the service delivery system. How can quality be designed into the service? The answer to this question lies in the nature of services being offered to the consumers. Quality customer service is an action-oriented activity which requires immediate corrective measures when nonconformance occurs.

Achieving Quality Customer Service

Quality services are very difficult for customers to evaluate before the fact. Services are intangible and consumed simultaneously with production. This presents companies with the challenge to evaluate the quality of service before it actually happens because quality-inspection intervention between the customer and the contact employee is not an option as in manufacturing. Service "with a smile" used to be just enough to satisfy most customers. But due to constant changes in the global marketplace and the competitive environment, companies must differentiate themselves in the marketplace by offering a "service guarantee." Unlike a product warranty which promises to repair or replace the faulty item, service guarantees typically offer the unhappy customer a refund, discount, or free service.

The Service Encounter Triad

One of the unique characteristics of customer service is the active participation of the customer in the service provision process. It is safe to say that every moment of truth involves an interaction between the customer and the service provider; each has a role to play in an environment staged by the company in the process formulation. The service encounter triad shown in Figure 1.2 captures the relationships between the three parties in the service encounter and suggests possible sources of conflict. To control service delivery, company managers must impose rules and procedures on the contact personnel to limit their autonomy and discretion when serving customers.

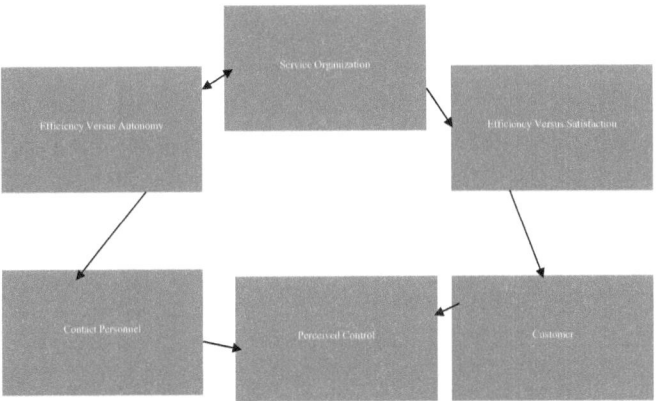

Figure 1.2: The Service Encounter Triad.

The managers of for-profit service organizations have an interest in delivering quality customer service as efficiently as possible to protect their companies' bottom-line and remain as competitive as possible. On the other hand, non-profit service organizations might substitute effectiveness for efficiency, but they still must operate under the limits imposed by their respective organizations' budgets.

Encounter Dominated by the Service Organization

It is very important to note that in order to be efficient and, perhaps to follow a cost leadership strategy; an organization may standardize the quality of service delivery by imposing strict operating procedures and, thus, severely limit the discretion of the contact personnel. If this strategy is followed, the customers are presented with few standard service options from which to choose, and personalized services are not available. Many franchise services such as McDonald's, Discount Tires, and Jiffy Lube have been successful with a structural organization and environment which dominates the service encounter. Much of their success has resulted from teaching customers what not to expect from their service; however, much of the frustration that customers experience with other institutions, labeled pejoratively as "bureaucracies," is the result of contact personnel having no autonomy to deal with individual customer's needs. Contact personnel in such organizations may sympathize with the customers but are forced to go "by the book," and their job satisfaction is diminished in the process.

Contact Personnel-Dominated Encounter

In general, service personnel try to limit the scope of the service encounter to reduce their own stress in meeting demanding customers. When contact personnel are placed in an autonomous position, they may perceive themselves as having a significant degree of control over customers. The customer is expected to place considerable trust in the contact person's judgment because of the service provider's perceived expertise. The relationship between a patient and a physician can best illustrate the shortcomings of the contact personnel-dominated encounter. The patient, who is not even referred to as a "customer," is placed in a subordinate position with no control over the encounter. Furthermore, an allied organization, such as a hospital in this case, is subjected to tremendous demands placed on it by individual staff physicians with no regard for matters of efficiency.

Customer-Dominated Encounter

It is very important to note that the extremes of standardized and customized services represent opportunities for customers to control the encounter. In the case of standardized services, self-service is an opting that gives customers complete control over the limited services provided. For example, at a self-service gas station that is equipped with a credit card reader, the customer need not interact with anyone. The result can be very efficient and satisfying to the customer who needs or desires very little service. For customized service such as legal defense in a criminal case, however, all the organization's resources may be needed, at great cost in efficiency.

Be that as it may, a satisfactory and effective customer service encounter should balance the need for control by all three participants. The organization's need for efficiency to remain economically viable can be satisfied when contact personnel are trained properly and the customer's expectations and role in the delivery process are communicated effectively.

The Customer

Every purchase of any product and/or service is an event of some importance for the customer, whereas the same transaction usually is routine for the service provider. The emotional involvement that is associated with the routine purchase of gas at self-service station or an overnight stay at a motel is minor, but thinks of the very personal and dramatic roles played by a customer taking an exotic vacation or seeking medical treatment. As it turns out, it is very difficult for the bored contact personnel, who see hundreds of customers weekly, to maintain a corresponding level of emotional commitment.

In the service encounter, both the service provider and the customer have roles to play in transacting the service. The competitive business environment in the global marketplace has brought about the need to provide quality customer service, and as such, society has defined specific tasks for customers to perform, such as the procedure required for cashing checks at a bank. Diners in some restaurants may assume a variety of productive roles, such as assembling their meals and carrying them to the table in the cafeteria, serving themselves at a salad bar, or busing their own tables. In each case, the customer has learned a set of behaviors that is appropriate for the situation. As it turns out, the customer is participating in the service delivery as a partial employee with a role to play and is following a script that is defined by societal norms or implied by the particular design of the services offered.

Customers possess a variety of scripts which are learned for use in different service encounters. Following the appropriate script allows both the customer and the service provider to predict the behaviors of each other as they play out their respective roles. Acceptance of new technology that replaces the human service encounter can take time while customers learn the new script. When customers learn their new script and grow to appreciate the reduced checkout lines in stores, the dedicated attendant might no longer be needed and the full benefit of the self-checkout investment will be realized. Teaching customers new roles can be facilitated if the transition becomes a logical modification of the past behaviors. Public acceptance of the Windows operating system for the PCs can be attributed to the fact that all applications share the same interface; thus, only one script must be learned.

Customers can be classified by their service expectations and attitudes. Service customers are in most cases, motivated to look for services much as they would for products; whereas, their expectations govern their shopping attitudes. Those who have the need for control are candidates for self-service options. Viewing customers as co-producers suggests the use of customer "scripts" that facilitate the service delivery and provide some behavioral predictability in the encounter. It goes without saying that the service encounter is viewed as a triad, with the customer and contact personnel both exercising control over the service process in an environment defined by the service organizations. The importance of flexibility in meeting customer needs has prompted many organizations to empower their personnel to exercise more autonomy in order to provide quality customer service.

Technology in the Service Encounter

The competitive environment in the global marketplace, the advances in communications and information technology are having a profound effect on ways customers interface with service providers. For instance, the Internet and airport kiosks have changed the expectations and behavior of airline passengers. Customers no longer need to wait on hold to reach a reservation associate or wait in line at the airline counter to receive a boarding pass.

Be as it may, technology has brought about greater challenges and altered how companies deal with customers. Customer service management software programs track and analyze data and customer feedback, thereby making information easier for companies to understand. By using the technological program to improve customer services, companies become better equipped to deliver quality products and services which customers want and market them more effectively.

When it comes to technological advancement, companies want more, more, more, and more again. Day by day, there are not only updated versions of old technologies on the market, but there are also new inventions coming along all the time. A few years ago, who could have imagined the tablet? Now, it is an indispensable piece of technology for many operations. A majority of companies use this technology to improve productivity, communication, or some other functions aimed at meeting customers' expectations. Very often, the incredible advances made aren't fully leveraged as customer communications tools, whether at the front end or the back end. New products can help improve your business' bottom line, and it makes sense to implement them at all stages to make for a more convenient customer experience. There's no single best answer when it comes to customer preferences. Some want to speak with a call center agent; others want to perform self-service tasks using a mobile app. And a significant and growing group of consumers want it both ways. They want to perform self-service tasks on an app and connect to an agent (without having to hold) when an issue can't be resolved using other channels.

In today's competitive business environment, how do companies give the customers what they want/need? The proliferation of devices and the rise of empowered consumers who demand flexible, fast and fiercely personal customer service makes this harder than ever. Mobile apps, intelligent self-service IVR systems, services powered by cutting-edge speech recognition technology and natural language understanding – or all of the above? The data shows the way. You must give customers choices and with options that are in tune with their lifestyles and life stages, and built to deliver the fast, personal, and convenient customer service that they genuinely appreciate.

How to Build Customer Trust and Loyalty through Technology

These days, technology is everywhere. Technology affects just about everything the modern human being does, and it even leaves its prints in the business world. One example of this is the way that technology works towards building better customer loyalty towards your business. In order to build customer loyalty through technology, it is crucial for businesses to be interactive with their customers, as well as efficient in delivering assistance. Here are some ways that modern-day technology allows companies to achieve these levels of responsiveness and efficiency and, as a result, build customer loyalty:

Live Chat Features

Live chat features are a great way for businesses to be more interactive with their customers. Live chat features are chat windows on websites that customers can use to speak to representatives from the company that the website belongs to or is associated with. Even though live chat features may not seem very effective at first glance, consumers are given immediate access to the assistance they need, and this help is delivered in seconds. This is extremely important to consumers, and this does wonders for building their customer loyalty.

Social Media Customer Service

In the past decade, social media outlets have taken their places in the technological world and in the lives of customers. Social media is always around us, and it is always affecting how any business runs. It is an important part of how the public views, interacts with, and feels about a company. To not use social media for customer service or for getting to know customers would be a great disadvantage to any company. For this reason, many businesses use social media customer service to their advantage to build customer trust and loyalty. In the past decade, social media outlets have taken their places in the technological world and in the lives of customers. Social media is always around us, and it is always affecting how any business operates. It is an important part of how the public views, interacts with, and feels about a company. To not use social media for customer service or for getting to know customers would be a great disadvantage to any company. For this reason, many businesses use social media customer service to their advantage to build customer trust and loyalty. Providing a support button on Facebook in order to be friendly and provide help to customers. Social media customer service is all about companies being more interactive with customers, while also increasing the efficiency of the business in the eyes of the consumers. As a result of this responsiveness, customers are able to experience businesses on a more personal level while receiving the assistance they need, thus building better customer loyalty towards a company which is utilizing social media.

Customer Support Software

Customer support software is one of many help desk solutions that businesses utilize. Support software exists in order to help customers and businesses alike, and is a great storage device for customer data.

Through Customer Support Software, customers are able to get the help they need from companies, therefore building their customer loyalty to a company even more. This also makes customers feel as if though their comments and questions are valued, and they will appreciate that they are not being ignored. Customers' time and opinions are valuable to the progress and improvement of a company, and customer support software allows businesses to utilize these resources rather than waste them. Companies are able to address complaints and concerns using this advanced software, and customers are able to get the results they want and need from the businesses that they depend on every single day to meet their needs.

As technology evolves, so do the many ways companies reach their customers-ideally, with better innovative ideas. Will new, and more improved technologies help companies keep their connection with customers personal, and if so, how do they avoid sacrificing provision of services for efficiency?

To find out, I asked 11 start-up entrepreneurs what they think the future of real-time communication technology will look like for their businesses around the globe. Here is what they had to say:

1- Instant Messaging Will Be A Game-Changer

As the competition in the global marketplace continues to change, communication will become more on demand and permission-based. Instant messaging will become a game-changer in the business world and will replace e-mails because they are quite faster and allow for an instant response. Currently, there are too many e-mails and unsolicited calls happening.

2- Communication Will Take an Omni-Device Approach

As technology continues to evolve, consumers globally will move across devices more frequently. Whether interactions happen while consumers are in front of their desktops at work, running in between meetings with their iPhones or sitting on the couch with iPad and watching TV, brands will need to access and optimize these interactions with consumers accordingly. Applying pattern recognition, technology will continue to evolve, optimize and improve each individual's content based on the time of day, location and device type.

3- The Physical World Will Be Used to Reach Customers

As technology gets better at interpreting the physical world around all people through augmented reality, RFID, geolocation, etc., and as speech recognition continues to evolve to a basic functional lexicon (Siri and Google), we expect to be able to literally talk to the objects, find out more about them and then connect to people regarding those objects. Whether it is stores, products, and landmarks, the physical world will be interpreted to create real-time conversion.

4- Current Platforms Will Further Improve Customer Engagement

An expansion of current platforms such as Skype is likely, and savvy small business owners will incorporate Skype (as well as other services) into their strategy to further improve customer engagement. One viable and promising idea is the expansion of live video chat. The ability to have a customer call in and receive information and product demonstrations from an actual person via video is expected to serve business exceptionally well.

5- Brands Will Use Online Platforms to Listen to Customers

Brands used to work on marketing programs for months before launching their messages to the business world. Currently, brands need to learn to adapt to real-time communications which means that every brand should be listening to its customer base in order to find relevant messaging and engagement opportunities.

6- Customers Will Talk To Brands with One Click

Talking to a company and other website users will become as simple as a click of a button. This kind of communication will rely less on phone numbers and more on Internet-based communication technologies. WebRTC is a great example of an emerging technology that is making this possible.

7- Brands Will Deliver Instant Gratification

With the combination of wearable technology, faster data aggregation and processing and consumers sharing their desires more openly, major brands will focus on delivering instant gratification. Brands will compete by delivering both customized messaging and offers at the exact time of customer demand.

8- The Timing of Messages Will Be Optimized

Our computers and phones capture a great deal of information regarding how and when we interact with these devices, and advertising entities are going to use this information more and more to optimize the timing of each delivery. Habits and calendars will help personalize opportunities which will improve how companies compete in the global marketplace.

9- Brands Will Use More Local Targeting

In communication, it is very essential to be reaching the right market segment with the message. As technology continues to evolve, brands will get better at using services that allow targeted local promotions to reach more relevant audiences. For instance, a promotion in Oklahoma City will not do a company much good if the people in the City of Houston see it. Hint: use Facebook's location-targeting tools for a company's page update.

10- Consumers Will Determine the Offers They Receive

Real-time communication is useless if it interrupts dinner and serves something people do not want. Customers, not brands, will determine the types of offers they receive based on category, frequency, and service requests. Communication that is customized to meet customer's interests is really in the best interest of brands-a safeguard against wasted marketing investments and negative customer engagement.

Dr. Bob L Ssekyanzi, PhD.

11- Brands Will Need the Right Context

Real-time communication technologies necessitate real-world context. In the future it will not be enough for brands to reach customers at the right time because they will need the right message as well. Matching message and timing requires smart data collection and technology to really personalize each communication with each consumer at scale. Having context that feels real and human will be key to brands successfully reaching customers in real time.

It is very important to note that the ultimate goal of an organization in terms of its customer interaction is to generate loyalty and patronage. There is no better way to do that than to offer quality products and services and to be responsive to customers. But as new technologies come to the market, it is easier for companies to provide customer service through channels which interact with customers and the complexity of those interactions.

As far as technology and customer service are concerned, change will continue, and continue to accelerate at an exponential rate. Looking back, ten years ago, a $200 computer had the equivalent computing power of an insect brain. Today, the same priced computer has the computing power of a mouse. In ten years, it will be the equivalent of one human brain. The advances that lie ahead are yet more staggering. Due to the intense competition in the global marketplace, companies should not make the fatal mistake of waiting for stability. Leaders must embrace continuous development and actively look forwards for new opportunities. Innovative organizations can move quickly ahead, adapting to avoid challenges, capitalizing on growth areas and eroding the market share of traditional competition.

The Emergency of Self-Service Concept

Self-service concept means offering customers and employees the tools and information needed to find answers to their questions and have a better experience with a product or service. Self-service experiences are often called "portals," a term which refers to a webpage that serves as a gateway to a specific topic or set of information.

What is a self-service portal?

A self-service portal is a website with resources that help users resolve service needs and find related information on their own. Self-service portals typically fall into one of two categories: customer self-service or employee self-service. It's not at all uncommon for a single company to offer both customer and employee self-service portals, and while the content and user experience will obviously vary dramatically between the two, both may be built using the same technology.

At a high level, any self-service portal should offer content and functionality to help users address common needs efficiently and without outside help such as the kiosk at the airport where customers can self-check-in efficiently. **(See Figure: 1.3).** The specifics of which common needs are addressable without outside help will, of course, vary greatly from company to company. A software company that caters to engineers might expect a high level of technical aptitude from its users, and so offers fairly complex solutions on its self-service portal.

What is customer self-service?

Customer self-service portals are designed to help consumers request services, find information, and resolve issues related to a company's products or services. Customer portal software often combines user-searchable knowledge bases with basic administrative functionality. The knowledge base part of a customer self-service portal might contain one or more FAQs; a browseable and searchable database of topics, articles, and tutorials; and a Q&A section where users pose questions for employees and community experts to address. Sometimes Q&As are set up as part of user forums to facilitate ongoing, in-depth product discussions and knowledge exchange.

On the administrative side, customer self-service functionality can range from simple password resets to software downloads and basic technical configuration processes. Sophisticated self-service systems can leverage a sort of triage system that points basic service requests to self-serve solutions while routing more complex problems to a human service agent.

It is very important to point out that service has migrated from human interaction to substitution of machines for service employees or, whenever feasible, to anywhere-anytime electronic service. This trajectory is in many ways similar to the past experience in the agricultural and manufacturing sectors of the economy where human labor has been driven out of the production process by technological advancement. For example, the introduction of the airport check-in kiosks by airlines provided customers with place-and-time convenience. However, services that can be digitized and delivered via the Internet, such as entertainment, information, and training, represent new opportunities for self-service technology (SST).

By definition, high-touch services such as health care, fire fighting, and dentistry remain immune to self-service, but some inroads are in the offing. For example, a patient at home can use a blood pressure machine to record heart activity that can be sent by either telephone, or e-mail to a remote receiver in the doctor's office.

With customer expectations rising and business offerings becoming more complex, companies must expand their levels of customer service, but face pressure to reduce costs in all areas of operation. The ability to improve service quality, while remaining cost effective, is heavily reliant on the company's ability to adopt and integrate effective self-service customer care alternatives.

According to Hof, Robert D., (1999), a key dimension of future autonomous self service will be visual, as virtual assistants move from traditional text-based understanding to image processing, and then to full visual interactions. Powered by Computer Vision technology, these hyper-advanced visual assistants will be trained using massive data sets of images of real customer issues, positioning them to see, interpret and influence our environments. They'll be able to visually guide us through almost any process, pointing out exactly what we need to do using video with Augmented Reality instructions on our smart device screens.

With customers preferring to use machines to get their services instead of interacting with an assisted service worker self-service is growing exponentially in all areas of retail, travel and hospitality, restaurants, healthcare and banking environments. It is estimated that by 2023 (Hof, Robert, D., 1999) the global self-service technology market will generate a market value of USD 32 billion, growing at a CAGR (compound annual growth rate) of 13%.

All in all, given the trend we are watching, the simple fact is; people enjoy using self-service options because the technology makes life more efficient. As the demand for self-service technologies continues to rise businesses will need to provide their clients with the resources that empower them with the ability to create services that are independent of immediate staff member participation or risk being left behind.

Figure: 1.3
The convenience of the airport check-in kiosk is very much appreciated by business travelers.

The proliferation of self-service has many implications for society as time goes by. Low-wages, unskilled, non-value-added service jobs are bound to disappear as technology advances. The emergency of self-service sector means that the growth in service jobs will be limited to highly skilled (e.g., health care), intellectual (e.g., professional), and creative (e.g., entertainment) pursuits.

Re-engineering Customer Service

Readiness to Embrace New Technology

Technology readiness refers to a person's propensity to embrace and use new technologies for accomplishing the goals in his/her life, whether at home, work or in-transit. Research on people's reactions to technology with regard to customer service identified eight (8) technology-related paradoxes: (a) Control/Chaos; (b) Freedom/Enslavement; (c) New/Obsolete; (d) Competence/Incompetence; (e) Efficiency/Inefficiency; (f) Fulfills/Creates Needs; (g) Assimilation/Isolation; and, (h) Engaging/Disengaging.

All the above paradoxes imply that technology triggers both positive and negative feelings as far as the concept of customer service is concerned. For example, the paradox competence/incompetence can facilitate feelings of intelligence and efficacy, or lead to feelings of ignorance and ineptitude.

The implications for organizational managers who are tasked with the introduction of new technology in order to improve customer service are two-fold. First, what is the overall level of readiness of the customer base affected by the new technology-based service? Once this level of readiness is clearly assessed, the extent and appropriate technology to implement, the pace of implementation, and support needed to assist customers will be realized. Second, understanding the technology readiness of the company's associates is extremely important for making the right choices in terms designing, implementing, and managing the associate interface. The issue of technology readiness is especially important for contact associates to whom customers may turn for assistance when problems arise. Organizational employees who rate high on both interpersonal skills and technology readiness are most likely to be good candidates for tech-support roles.

Dr. Bob L Ssekyanzi, PhD.

Customer Service and Technological Innovation Services

As companies become very familiar with the emerging technological innovation services in the global marketplace, companies must be prepared to prepare their workers for new tasks and to provide input into the technology interface design (e.g., will typing skill be required, or will employees just point and click?). For customer services, the impact of new technology is not limited to the back office. It could require a change in the role that customers play in the service delivery process.

Ways to Improve Customer Service through Technology

When it comes to providing service, one would assume that companies wouldn't need to be told that customer service is one of the most important parts of what they do. It is without a doubt that without companies providing quality customer service, it is impossible to retain and acquire customers for their business ventures.

It is very important to note that in order for companies to keep customer service fresh and accommodating, companies must stay up-to-date and offer convenient services their customers can connect with. Implementing new and up-to-date technology, for example, is a great way to improve quality customer service. Although technology is an expensive investment for most companies, it can be a key element for companies to connect with customers on a deeper level. The following are five ways for companies to connect with customers through technology:

(1) Appropriate Communication

With the competitive environment in the global marketplace, companies are challenged to improve the way they communicate with customers through the technological advancements.

(2) Empathy

One of the biggest complaints (Pauline, Ashenden, 2015) customers have, when they raise an issue with a company, is that customer service associates/agents do not show sufficient understanding or empathy for their plight. In contrast, when associates/agents apologize and demonstrate that they realize that there is a problem that is causing an inconvenience, customer satisfaction rises. This is even the case if the issue cannot be resolved immediately through factors outside the associates/agents' control.

Over the years, customer service studies have shown that HYPERLINK "http://www.eptica.com/blog/importance-empathy-customer-service-interactions" the number one reason customers get frustrated with customer service reps is their lack of understanding. Consumers feel that representatives are uncaring and apathetic to their plights.

In reality, the representatives are simply doing their jobs by following the protocols set by their companies. Fortunately, thanks to the power of technology, companies can rewrite their policies in order to allow for greater empathy. They can encourage more human interaction on the phone, and set a precedent as a caring company through digital marketing, SMS messaging, social media, chat, and more.

(3) Availability

There's really no such thing as 9 to 5 customer service anymore, and those who still operate in that time frame are likely falling behind. Businesses now have the capacity to be available anytime - whether through a late-night chat or social engagement - and those who want to stand out will utilize these services.

Organizations can also be available anywhere, anytime by utilizing all forms of communication, including email, forms, multiple social networks, chat boxes, 24-hour customer service, and SMS messaging. Giving customers the option to contact you whenever they want and however they want offers a freedom that customers value and can't find with every business.

(4) Self-Reliant Customers

A lot of people don't like to ask for help, so teaching self-reliance through technology is an important part of great customer assistance. Now that consumers can access information through multiple avenues, the customer service lines are much shorter. Businesses with well-functioning websites can provide a wealth of knowledge for customers, including contact information, chat boxes, operating hours, store policies, and business descriptions.

This can also act as an authority in a certain niche, giving your brand more credibility. Through blog posts, webinars, podcasts, videos, and other sources of posted media, businesses can show customers how to help themselves. With the help of these information sources, 67 percent of customers are now able to find the answers to questions by themselves.

(5) *Social Media Connection*

One of the greatest inventions technology has delivered for business-customer relations is social media. Thanks to this little gem, customers and businesses can now connect 24/7 - without being overbearing. Through sharing blog posts, webinars, infographics, how-to videos, and more, companies can connect with their customers in a way that customers prefer, without being too pushy. It allows customers to come to you, which is the best way to acquire and retain your customer base.

Customer Service Technology

There are a few major areas in which technology now is able to help provide key advantages to businesses in engendering customer loyalty by improving customer service:

- Websites. Providing areas on your website where customers can answer their own questions or seek answers from others.
- E-mail. Using e-mail as a way to improve customer service and more quickly respond to certain needs or help requests.
- Communications. Unifying communications so that you know that the customer who left a voice mail also sent an e-mail with the same request a few days ago.
- Software. Better managing customer relationships with more sophisticated data-gathering tools, such as customer relationship management software.

Giving Customers What They Want, and the time frame of When They Want It

The goal of your business in terms of its customer interactions is the generate loyalty. There's no better way to do that than to offer quality products and services and to be responsive to your customers. But as new technologies have come to market to make it easier for businesses to provide customer service, they may also be increasing the number of channels through which you interact with customers and the complexity of those interactions. Accenture, the technology consulting firm, suggests that businesses that want to use technology to raise the quality of their customer service focus on the following:

- Data management and analytics. Using data collected from customer to analyze their shopping preferences.
- Insight-driven marketing. Gaining insights into your business from customer data so you can more effectively target marketing.
- Marketing automation. Streamlining and automating business processes to improve efficiency and keep costs low.
- Self-service optimization. Finding ways for customers to interact with your business when they want.
- Workforce effectiveness. Encouraging your staff to embrace new ways improving customer treatment by providing tools and training to deliver better service

Customer Characteristics

It is very important to note that the demographic and psychographic characteristics of targeted customer segments will form the basis for channel design decisions. Answers to questions such as what customers need-as well as why, when, and how they buy- are used to determine ways in which the products should be made available to generate a competitive advantage.

Customer characteristics may cause products to be distributed through two different types of channels. Many industrial goods marketers' sales, such as those of Caterpillar, are handled by individual dealers, except when the customer might be the central government or one of its entities, in which case sales are direct from the company itself. Additionally, primary target customers may change from one market to another. For example, in Japan, McDonald's did not follow the U.S. pattern of locating restaurants in the suburbs. The masses of young pedestrians that flood Japanese cities were more promising than affluent but tradition-minded car owners in the suburbs.

Customer Service Levels

The level of customer service denotes the responsiveness that inventory policies permit for any given situation. It is safe to note, therefore, that customer service is a management-determined constraint within the logistics system. A customer service level of 100 percent could be defined as the ability to fill all orders within a set time-for example, two or three days. If within two or three days 80 percent of the orders can be filled, the customer service level is only 80 percent (Rick, 2006). The choice of customer service level for the company has a major impact on the inventories needed to meet customer demands. Customer service levels should not be oriented primarily around cost or customary domestic standards. Rather, the level of customer service chosen for use should be based on customer expectations encountered in each market segment.

Because customer service levels are costly, the goal should not be the highest customer level possible but rather quality customer service possible. Different customers have different priorities. Some customers are prepared to pay a premium for speed. In industrial marketing, for example, even an eight-hour delay may be unacceptable for delivery of a crucial product component, since it may mean a shutdown of the production process. Other companies may put a higher value on flexibility, and other companies may see low cost as the most important issue. Flexibility and speed are expensive, so it is wasteful to supply them to customers who do not value them highly. The higher product prices associated with higher customer service levels may reduce the competitiveness of a company's product.

What New Technologies will Improve Customer Service?

As machine technology once changed an agricultural economy into an industrial economy, today's information technology is transforming the industrial economy into a service economy. The availability of computers and global communication technologies had created industries for collecting, processing, and communicating information. Today, more people in the world can be in instant communication with everyone else, and this revolution is changing the way businesses deal with customers on every level of service.

Providing the required services to the customers especially in this globally competitive business environment is quite challenging to businesses. Either interacting personally or through information processes, customers' perception concerning a market offering is built upon the ability of the service provider to attractively convince their various target market segments.

Technological Innovation in Customer Service

All things considered, innovation, by no means is a destroyer of tradition; thus, it requires careful planning in order to ensure business success. By all means, the productivity benefits of new technology changes the nature of work. Any introduction of new technology in all cases should include employee familiarization so as to prepare associates for new tasks and to provide input into the technology interface design (e.g., will typing skills be required, or will associates just point and click?). It is very essential to note that for services, the impact of new technology is not limited to the back office. It requires a change in the role customers play in the service delivery process **(See Figure 1.4).**

Consumers' reaction to the new technology, determined through focus groups or interviews, can provide input into the design to avoid future problems of acceptance, (e.g., consider the need for surveillance cameras at automated teller machines).

Image: iStock and the competitive business enviroment

Figure: 1.4 Customer Service and Application of Technological Innovations

When it comes to customer service, new technologies are raising consumer expectations and companies will pay the price if they don't respond on time to implement processes which aim at delivering exceptional quality products and services to their customers.

Dr. Bob L Ssekyanzi, PhD.

Customer relations play a key role in the success or failure of a business. Strong relationships build brand loyalty and encourage repeat business, while poor customer service can drive buyers to your competitors. As the competition in the global marketplace continues to intensify and with no ending in sight, technological innovations have made it easy for businesses to interact with customers, particularly for small businesses that may not have the funds for traditional marketing and advertising techniques. Technology now allows consumers to reach a company at a time that's convenient for them, not just during business hours. Using email or Web submission forms, buyers can share feedback or ask questions about products or services. Electronic communication is also cheaper and faster for both parties, and the convenience factor may encourage more customers to interact with their favorite businesses.

Technology can also help companies streamline operations, reduce staff and processes, and cut costs internally, which can then be passed on to the consumer in the form of lower prices. Since many consumers actively seek out value pricing, this strategy serves as an effective way of building customer relations.

Technology has become an indispensable part of modern living. From mobile devices to smart phones to personal computers, all the way up to ads on LED screens and social media, it can literally be found in practically every corner of our lives. It goes without saying that businesses have tried to find ways to improve their customer service through the use of technology, so much so that customer service has become incomplete without it.

Technology is no longer just a nice-to-have tool, but an integral part of every business arsenal, especially for smaller enterprises with stretched resources and budgetary constraints.

In order to understand just how important technology is to customer service at this modern age, the following five reasons can help in understanding the importance of technology from a business perspective with regard to customer service:

1. Technology enables faster and better service that customers demand

It's a byproduct of technological innovation. Customers expect your business to at least have your own website, where they can know more about what you offer and answer questions about your business, products or services. They expect you to have an email were they can reach you, and they want you to answer questions and concerns promptly on your social media accounts. They want to be able to reach you via multiple devices and interact act with you via mobile phone.

Not only do they expect you to have an online presence, they also demand seamless integration among your online accounts and customer service touch points. And why not? It should be relatively easy for you to check your Facebook account or coordinate with a customer service agent they spoke with about an issue or question. Customers don't want to waste time repeating something they've said before, and expect you to be on top of any issues they have with your product.

2. Technology helps you to improve customer experience

Technology gives you the ability to interact with customers on a regular basis. Don't miss this opportunity to gather as much feedback and customer insight as you can to inform your next marketing campaign or to introduce improvements to your current products or service. Encourage active engagement with your online followers. Reach out to your target audience. Find out exactly what they want. Don't take criticisms in a negative light, but as an opportunity to improve.

You can also use analytics or data gathering software to gain buyer behavior without even having to ask customers point blank what they want. The online footprints they leave can also give you valuable insight into what motivates them and why they're willing to purchase from you, or a competitor.

Technology enables you to delight customers with thoughtful gestures. For example, food trucks that offer credit card payments or other payment options can easily set you apart from your competition. It's an unexpected but much appreciated feature that makes it easier for clients to buy from you. As the abilities of digital technologies develop, customers have started to expect new standards of excellence, performance, and pretty much about everything in-between.

3. Technology helps accelerate customer loyalty

By now you should be aware that your primary goal in customer service is to generate loyalty. Focus on your current customers and find out what will motivate them to keep coming back to you. Technology can help you create loyalty programs, and once it is set up properly, it allows for automation that helps form a lasting, continuous relationship with your target customers. As long as you continue to pay attention to what they want, and implement their feedback promptly, they'll stick around and even help spread the word about your business. They'll be your unofficial brand ambassadors, ready to promote your product to their own social circle and thus, gain more customers for you.

Because of its ubiquity, businesses that don't leverage on technology can quickly be left behind by competition. Technology has encroached every aspect of modern living, and using it to enhance your customer service strategy will benefit not only the clients you're serving, but your financial health as well.

4. Increased automation

Contact centers are increasingly using voice recognition and call-routing technologies. The customer can speak to a computer or press keys that will route him or her to the appropriate department to handle the request. Call routing improves customer service by allowing the customer to go straight to the person that can handle his or her needs. This saves the customer from repeating the request to numerous representatives and ultimately saves time for the customer and saves money for the organization. Research technologies and consultants can help automate routine processes. Visit similar businesses to understand how they have implemented technology in their operating processes. Interview other businesses to discover how automation has impacted their business positively and negatively.

5. Customer empowerment

Technology also empowers the customer. With technology, the customer can get what is needed from the company. Self-checkout lines have become popular in retail outlets. The customer goes into the store to get what is needed and can check out without interacting with the company's associates. The customer is satisfied because he or she can quickly get exactly what is needed, purchase and pay for the item without a long wait. The customer may also choose not to self-checkout and prefer to use a cashier line. This, again, increases customer service because he or she has an option. The customer has control over how he or she interacts with the organization. Look to see what the company can allow the customers to access themselves. When evaluating, be prepared to change or completely eliminate some processes. Simplify the processes to make it easier for the customer. Additionally, the following 5 (five) technological concepts can play an important role in improving customer service:

1. Use Emails to notify customers about new offers and deals:

It is human nature people want to buy at a lower cost, whenever people see a 50% discount on any product or products being sold at 0.99 cents, they will be encouraged to rush and buy while the product is still on discount. So as a business, you can use this human weakness, by tailoring electronic HTML emails with products or services on discount, suggest deals which can expire in a specific period of time, this will create trust and desire to buy on instant. Offering these special deals and discounts to your customers will make them feel cared for. There are good examples of companies that have used their information technology process to improve customer service. When you purchase a product from online companies that apply the innovative ideas and resources of technology, your interests are tracked whenever you go back to their online store, and they use web cookies to gather data about you, the information they collect is used to tailor shopping deals and suggest items related to your previous purchase at a lower price.

Figure: 1.5 Sale and Discount signs

2. Collect information and data about your customers:

As a business you can use Information technology to collect data about your customers, so that you tailor your services basing on their needs. A business can serve its customers by delivering the best service or product on time at an affordable cost. Their some companies which have concentrated on creating the best service or product for their customers and this has saved them money they would have spent in creating expensive persuasive adverts. As a business, it makes no sense to create a very beautiful persuasive advert, yet your service or products cannot fulfill customer needs and expectations. To collect this data, you can set up a website which loads a survey form when ever its loaded, or provide a help section on your website where your customers can file complaints and concerns about your service or product. Listen to what your customers are suggesting so that you serve them basing on their needs and expectations. In business, *it is not what you want; it is what your customers want.* You can use feedback tool like *uservoice.com* to get feedback from your users.

3. Have a customer care representative both on phone, email and social networks:

Make sure that you respond to customer requests on time. Avoid using auto responders or robots answering phones when customers call for support. Remember, you're not the only one in the market, your competitors will base on your weakness to gain competitive advantage. So it is very important to be available at all times when a customer needs your support. It is not expensive to have a well organized customer support team at work, simply dedicate someone experienced for that job and train them so that they know how to handle customers. For example, when it comes to email support, you can draft a template which a support representative will follow when replying a customer, if the issue is technical, let someone in the technical department handle the customer, also make sure that you create a support mail in your company name for example (support@yourcompanyname.com).

4. Make payment of services and products easier:

Now that you have listened to your customers, you have tailored the service or product for them. They like what you provide and its time to make an order. Make sure that this is one of the simplest things for them to do. Your mode of payment is part of customer service, provide various means of payment. For example, offline businesses can provide electronic visa card payment systems so that their clients can simply use their smart money cards to purchase products. Then for online businesses, you can use smart card electron payment services like *"VISA ELECTRON"*, and then also integrate other payment services like "PayPal". For security reasons, many online buyers have resorted to **PAYPAL** as their default mode of payment, since they do not have to expose their financial details on every website online. If a customer likes the service or product, they will want to buy it and they expect delivery to be fast. So if possible you can provide free delivery and shipment as a bonus.

5. Be known and trusted:

Let your customers know your location via your website. Before a customer decides to do business with you, they will do some background check on your company. In this case, you will have to show a location of your business by use of Google Maps, then you can as well show some decision makers profiles in the "**About Us**" section of your website. Let the support phone number and email be seen clearly and let customers who have used your service post testimonies to your website. The main advantage of these testimonies is to win confidence and trust among new customers.

It must be clearly pointed out that good customer service is the lifeblood of any business operation. You can offer promotions and slash prices to bring in as many new customers as you want, but unless you can get some of those customers to come back, your business won't be profitable for long.

Good customer service is all about bringing customers back. And about sending them away happy - happy enough to pass positive feedback about your business along to others, who may then try the product or service you offer for themselves and in their turn become repeat customers.

If you're a good salesperson, you can sell anything to anyone once. But it will be your approach to customer service that determines whether or not you'll ever be able to sell that person anything else. The essence of good customer service is forming a relationship with customers – a relationship that that individual customer feels that he would like to pursue.

How do we go about forming such a relationship? By remembering the one true secret of good customer service and acting accordingly; "You will be judged by what you do, not what you say."

I know these verges on the kind of statement that's often seen on a sampler, but providing good customer service is a simple thing. If you truly want to have good customer service, all you have to do is ensure that your business consistently follows the eight rules following:

- **Answer your customers' phone calls and be courteous.**

Get call forwarding or an answering service system. Hire staff if you need to. But make sure that someone is picking up the phone when someone calls your business. (Notice I say "someone". People who call want to talk to a live person, not a fake "recorded robot".) And then read How to Answer the Phone Properly to make sure that customers calling your business are thrilled with the way you answer the phone rather than put off **(See Figure 1.6).**

Figure: 1.6: More consumers are yelling when dealing with customer service.

Re-engineering Customer Service

- **Don't make promises you can't keep**

As far as customer service is concerned, keeping promises you have made to your customer in the process of providing services and product, is one of the most important rules for good and quality customer service. Reliability is one of the keys to any good relationship, and good customer service is by no means exception. If you promise your customers that a certain product will be available for them on Tuesday, make sure that the said product is available on Tuesday. Otherwise, don't promise what you cannot deliver. The same rule applies to customer appointments, deadlines, etc.. Think before you give any promise - because nothing annoys customers more than a broken promise.

When organizations keep promises and everybody wins. If you estimate delivery by the 15th, tell your customers that the product will arrive between the 15th and 17th. Then, if it arrives before the 15th, you will have a delighted customer. If the product arrives any time within the timeframe, you will have a happy and satisfied customer. That sure beats facing a disappointed customer if you set the expectation for the 15th and the product arrives on the 16th!

Figure: 1.7: Listen to your Customers

Is there anything more exasperating than telling someone what you want or what your problem is and then discovering that that person hasn't been paying attention and needs to have it explained again? From a customer's point of view, I doubt it. Can the sales pitches and the product babble. Let your customers talk and demonstrate to them that you are listening by making appropriate responses which aim at solving the problems they face.

How to Effectively Listen to Customers

1. Let the customer speak.

You can't listen to another person if you're speaking. So, in order to truly listen, your reps need to remain silent until the customer has finished explaining their problem. Even if they already know the solution, interrupting them makes your team look impatient. It's better to wait until the customer is done speaking as you never know what information they may have that could alter the case.

2. Stay humble and patient.

It can be frustrating to work with a customer who's new to your product or service. They don't know the basics, they fumble the terminology, and it feels like you need to hold their hand for every troubleshooting step. These are the cases where reps can mentally check-out and overlook costly details.

In these instances, it's important for reps to keep their cool and remain humble. Remember, there was a time where they were just as new to the product and they probably felt just as lost when they had questions. Every question is significant, so your team needs to value each one equally no matter how well the case is going **(See Figure 1.7).**

3. Engage with customers on their preferred channels.

The goal of customer service is to make people more comfortable with your business. Part of that is communicating with customers on channels that they prefer to work on. This requires your team to have an in-depth understanding of your customer base.

This is also an opportunity for customer service to align with marketing. Have service managers assess your customer personas and identify the channels that your customers use most.

For example, if you're targeting a Millennial audience, you may find that social media is their preferred communication channel. So, you can assign reps to your social media accounts to field questions that customers may pose. That way, you'll reduce friction in the customer's experience by meeting them on a channel they're already using.

4. Consider your body language.

You may think this tip is only for in-person customer service, but these practices can affect calls and chats as well. Body language is a major factor that shows whether or not you're listening to a customer. If your rep's body signals that they're uninterested or not paying attention, then they probably aren't listening to the customer.

And, that goes for phones and chats, too. Even if you're not directly facing the customer, your body language can still influence the interaction. For example, if you sit straight up at your desk and maintain a smile, you're naturally going to be more energetic and optimistic during a call.

5. Practice active listening.

Active listening is a communication approach that sales reps use to close deals. However, this method for interacting with customers translates perfectly to customer service.

Active listening places the focus on the customer's speech. Rather than scrambling to find a quick solution, it encourages reps to only think about what the customer is saying then repeat the problem back to them to ensure they fully understand the issue. This shows the customer that your rep is invested in the case and that they have a clear understanding of the problem.

Effective Customer Engagement Strategies

Customers are the lifeblood of your business. Whether you sell ebooks, software, consulting, coaching, or a physical product (e.g., clothing), without loyal customers, your ambitions and business aspirations are destined to fail.

Most companies tend to pay more attention to lead generation and customer acquisition and forget that until the ideal customer are effectively motivated and upgraded in their own state of mind and likely would switch to competitors is the quality of services and/or products do not meet their expectations. It is very important to note that the way customers are treated matters. Customers always look for a wonderful shopping experience.

According to Verint, Table 1.2, 61% of consumers would tell friends and family about their experiences, while 27% reported that they would sign up to the company's loyalty scheme.

Re-engineering Customer Service

People have a diminishing attention span. Since these people (customers) come from different sources, it's important to track engagement on both desktop and mobile devices.

According to a recent report from IMRG Calpgemini, "a total of 52% of web traffic to retail sites currently comes via smartphones and tablets."

More so, over a third (36%) of online sales are now completed on a smartphone or tablet device.

More customer interactions across channels and devices will give them a "welcome note" to remain loyal.

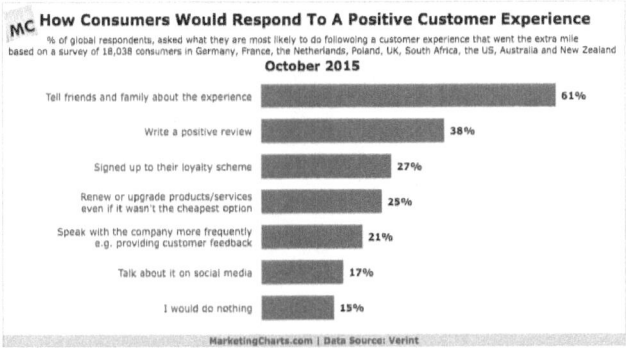

Table: 1.2: Use social media as an engagement tool and not simply a platform.

You're closer to reaching your personal peak, if only you can change your mindset about social media.

The rapidly evolving behavior of consumers in this age should impact your perception about social media marketing.

Social media is huge. As of July, 2015, the total worldwide population is 7.3 billion. And out of these, about 2.3 billion people are active social media users.

Use social media as an engagement tool and not simply a platform

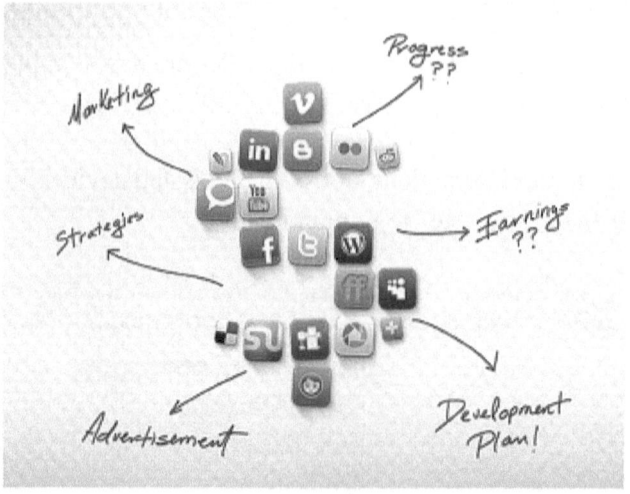

Figure: 1.8

Begin to see social media as a tool, not just a platform. This means that you can use the tool to connect, share, identify questions, research influencers and other experts, and create content that your fans will scream, "Wow, 've been looking for this!"

Most brands merely regard Facebook, Twitter, and other social media networks as platforms.

Engage customers with In-Product messaging

When it comes to product messaging (i.e., notifying your customers about your new product), there are several key channels that you can use.

Re-engineering Customer Service

According to Wikipedia (2016), in-product messaging means:

"Content, and related media delivered directly to a user's internet-connected device or software application, with the purpose of informing, gathering feedback from, engaging with, or marketing to that specific user or segment of users at often-higher engagement rates than other digital marketing and online marketing channels."

The part of this definition that you should consider critically is:

"Marketing to that specific user or segment of users."

From the definition, you can see that when you send targeted message to a segment of your users, you'll get higher engagement rates.

You should segment your email list. Because if you don't, you'll blindly send the same message to everyone.

Sadly, not everyone of your subscribers or ideal customers want your latest product or ebook.

Sending out of context emails will likely increase your customer's email fatigue.

The ideal approach is to message a specific segment of your customer base with the exact product/offer which they've indicated interest.

In-product messaging is a viable strategy to adopt, because there is a market fit, which is the direction correlation between product and market.

- **Train Your Associates how to Engage the customers**

Figure: 1.9 Employees/Associates Customer Engagement

Train your staff (if you have any) to be always helpful, courteous, and knowledgeable of the system and processes used in providing services and products.

Do it yourself or hire someone to provide training. Talk to your associates about good customer service and what it is/what it isn't regularly. Most importantly, give every associate enough information and power to make those small customer-pleasing decisions, so that they may never say, "I don't know, but so-and-so will be back at..."

If you apply the above mentioned simple rules consistently, your business will become known for its good customer service. And the best part? Over time good customer service will bring in more new customers than promotion and price slashing ever did!

Managing and Measuring Customer Satisfaction

Measuring customer satisfaction is a relatively new concept to many companies that have been focused exclusively on income statements and balance sheets. Companies now recognize that the new global economy has changed things forever. Increased

Re-engineering Customer Service

competition, crowded markets with little product differentiation and years of continual sales growth followed by two decades of flattened sales curves have indicated to today's sharp competitors that their focus must change.

Competitors that are prospering in the new global economy recognize that measuring customer satisfaction is the key **(See Figure 1.9).** Only by doing so can they hold on to the customers they have and understand how to better attract new customers. The competitors who will be successful recognize that customer satisfaction is a critical strategic weapon that can bring increased market share and increased profits.

Too many companies rely on outdated and unreliable measures of customer satisfaction. They watch sales volume. They listen to sales reps describing their customers' states of mind. They track and count the frequency of complaints. And they watch aging accounts receivable reports, recognizing that unhappy customers pay as late as possible—if at all. While these approaches are not completely without value, they are no substitute for a valid, well-designed customer satisfaction surveying program.

Conducting a customer satisfaction surveying program is a burden on the organization and its customers in terms of time and resources. There is no point in engaging in this work unless it has been thoughtfully designed so that only relevant and important information is gathered. This information must allow the organization to take direct action. Nothing is more frustrating than having information that indicates a problem exists but fails to isolate the specific cause. Having the purchasing department of a manufacturing firm rate the sales and service it received on its last order on a scale of 1 (poor) to 10 (excellent) would yield little about how to improve sales and service to the manufacturer.

The lesson is twofold. First, general questions are often not that helpful in customer satisfaction measurement, at least not without many other more specific questions attached. Second, the design of an excellent customer satisfaction surveying program is more difficult than it might first appear. It requires more than just writing a few questions, designing a questionnaire, calling or mailing some customers, and then tallying the results.

The most basic objective of a customer satisfaction surveying program is to generate valid and consistent customer feedback (i.e., to receive the voice of the customer, which can then be used to initiate strategies that will retain customers and thus protect the most valuable corporate asset—loyal customers).

As it's determined what needs to be measured and how the data relate to loyalty and repurchase, it becomes important to examine the mind-set of customers the instant they are required to make a pre-purchase (or repurchase) decision or a recommendation decision. Surveying these decisions leads to measures of customer loyalty. In general, the customer's pre-purchase mind-set will fall into one of three categories—rejection (will avoid purchasing if at all possible), acceptance (satisfied, but will shop for a better deal), and/or preference (delighted and may even purchase at a higher price).

This highly subjective system that customers themselves apply to their decisions is based primarily on input from two sources:

The customers' own experiences—each time they experience a product or service, deciding whether that experience is great, neutral, or terrible. These are known as "moments of truth."

Re-engineering Customer Service

The experiences of other customers—each time they hear something about a company, whether it's great, neutral, or terrible. This is known as "word of mouth."

There is obviously a strong connection between these two inputs. An exceptional experience leads to strong word-of-mouth recommendations. Strong recommendations influence the experience of the customer, and many successful companies have capitalized on that link.

The Concept of Customer Service as it relates to Technology

Customers want and need information regarding the services and products being offered. They want an easy way to get that information and connect with businesses. A mobile app is an exceptional and often must-have tool for businesses. According to Zetlin (2007), customers expect mobile apps to provide information while also allowing them interaction based on their need. When your product fails to deliver or a complication arises from its use, the first thing your customer wants is for you to solve the problem. Even if it is their lack of understanding how to use it, they need you to provide exceptional service to just fix it. That is not always a simple solution. In many cases, the first step to fixing a problem like this is to provide over-the-phone or over-the-internet support services. Some companies are known for providing exceptional tech service like this.

You may have noticed a few innovations in the way of customer service on various websites you've visited. Here's an overview of how you can use technology tools out there to streamline your customer service experience and gain new clients.

Virtual Customer Service: You've probably seen an animated person pop up when you visit some websites, or at least a text chat box appear, with a greeting from a virtual service rep. This is technology's version of the perky salesperson that greets you in a store, except you can ignore them if you want!

These are great ways to catch visitors to your site that may be looking for something in particular, or who may leave the site if they don't immediately find what they need. You can quickly assess the visitor's needs and help him right away. Additionally, for people who detest calling customer service only to sit on the phone for an hour, these are instant gratification tools that let customers get what they need immediately!

Blogs: If you don't know what a blog is by now, you're a rare species. Companies use blogs to tell customers and website visitors about new products, modifications of old products, and to address customer concerns. Many blogs operate in a forum manner, which means readers can leave comments. Say, for example, a reader leaves a post that talks about problems he/she is having installing your software on a Mac. You can reply to the blog for all to see with a solution. Blogs can keep your issues out in the open, where you can resolve them for the good of all your existing customers and prospective customers.

Real-time messaging will outpace email.

Email is dead, and long lives chat. Right? Well, yes and no. Just like video, customers expect you to be always on -- and most of them prefer to interact using chat than phone or email. Facebook Messenger as a channel for support has pushed us ahead light years! Now, you can converse with businesses in real-time, and Facebook will even show you their average responsiveness (and if that responsiveness is poor, forget even engaging at all).

Re-engineering Customer Service

This expectation of real-time messaging and responsiveness seeps into other media, too. It's not just the expectation on Facebook Messenger or Slack (either internally or with vendors), but on-site conversations and chat are all expected to be real-time, 1:1, and authentic. That's a big change from the world of asynchronous snail mail, and then email.

The world operates in synchronous time now -- so that means you need to amp up your communication technologies and strategies while still using email to share important documents and communications your customers will want to come back to again and again. HubSpot offers a shared inbox tool that allows all incoming messages from customers, across channels, to be collected and assigned in one place. Above all, technology, despite all its progress, cannot replace the most important qualities of human service representatives in the long run: emotionality and the ability to take responsibility. This is why qualified customer advisors are crucial for customer service – for example, when it comes to solving a problem with an angry customer in an empathetic and polite manner, or to picking up on subtle language and mood nuances in difficult conversations and replying accordingly. For this reason, personal customer service remains the first choice when it comes to solving complex problems.

Be it as it may, when it comes to empathy and personality, automated solutions don't lead to the goal – quite the contrary: In these cases, the customer will still perceive a "mechanical" solution as negative in the future, with corresponding consequences for the reputation of the company. In the future, the emotional and complex topics in particular will reach customer service representatives in the service center, which will increase the demands on their skills.

Dr. Bob L Ssekyanzi, PhD.

Understanding the Concept of Winning Customers in the Marketplace

In an environment of market economy circulated with competition, customers are hungry and continuously look for products and services that can meet their needs. Depending on the competition and personal needs, segments of customers select service providers using various criteria, but the most common criteria are:

- **Availability:** When choosing the service provider, customers think first of the availability of the product/service based on how accessible the service and/or product may be. For example, the use of ATMs by banks has nevertheless, created 24-hour availability of some banking services (i.e., service beyond the traditional "bankers' hours"). The use of 800-numbers and Websites by service firms facilitate the availability and accessibility to information and personal accounts 24 hours a day 7days a week (24/7).
- **Convenience:** The location of the service defines the convenience for customers who must travel to that location for service. For example, gas stations, fast food restaurants, and dry cleaners provide an example of services that must select locations on busy streets if they want to succeed.
- **Quality:** It is very important to note that service quality is a function of the relationship between customers' prior expectations of the products and services and their perception of the service/product experience, both during and after the fact. Unlike the product quality, service quality is judged by both the process of service delivery and the outcome of the service.
- **Safety:** The well-being and security of customers are very important considerations because in many ways, customer

service such as air travel and medicine, the customers are putting their lives in the hands of the service provider.

- **Speed:** Last but by no means least; speed is an important element of the customer service. How long must the customer wait for service? For emergency services such as fire and police protection, response time is the major criterion of performance. In other services, waiting sometimes may be considered a trade-off for receiving more personalized services, or in reduced rates.

Figure: 1.10: Customers in search of quality services and products

New technology is continuously emerging all around us, particularly in the world of the consumer market. Companies are seeing massive advertising space in social media like Facebook and blogs, and customers are increasingly using online platforms to shop, compare, recommend or review products and services. It is definitely safe to say that customers are becoming more tech-smart, and whilst it is thrilling to be able to see what our audiences want, it requires some shift in company approach, particularly when it comes to presentation and communication.

One area where this could not be truer is the realm of customer service. Customer service is the crucial yet frequently-overlooked asset of a company that is largely responsible for generating customer satisfaction, loyalty, and inevitably company turnover. Customer service should be a number one priority for every company and recognized as the genuine minefield for profit, not merely a necessary or formal-sounding 'add on' for the company's structure.

Technological equipments for better customer service
Figure: 2.0

Technology and social media need not be an overwhelming thing – they ought to be harnessed and exploited in order to provide the best customer service experience possible and smaller businesses in particular can benefit from this. Although new channels have made customer interactions more complex, they also create opportunity for better-controlled and more manageable onsets of heavy customer service demands.

Challenges of Adopting New Technology in Services

The real importance of technological business advancement is not in the emergence of new technology; rather, the importance is in the shift in customer behaviors toward products and services.

Re-engineering Customer Service

Because customers participate directly in the service delivery, the process is the product. Therefore, the success of technological innovations, particularly for the front office, depends on customer acceptance. The impact on customers is not always limited to a loss of personal attention. Customers also may need to learn new skills (e.g., how to operate a teller machine or pump gasoline), or they may have to forgo some benefits (e.g., loss of float through the use of electronic funds transfer).

The incentive to provide innovative customer service is hampered, however, because many ideas cannot be patented. One example is the idea of self-service in retailing. Much of the potential for technological and organizational progress can be found in the area of retailing. The prospective rewards for innovations are diminished, however, because the innovations may be freely imitated and quickly implemented by the competitive forces.

To meet future challenges in a sustainable way, customer service leaders must develop the capability to quickly identify, evaluate and invest in the right trends at the right time. For many organizations, this means acquiring or developing new talent that better understands digital technologies and how to apply them. Interestingly, (Rust, et al., 2002) many marketing and e-Commerce teams have already begun to seek out this kind of talent to meet their digital challenges. Social media managers, data scientists and growth hackers are some of the new job titles that are lining these teams. Service, sales and marketing teams should work together closely to leverage this talent across the entire customer journey.

In looking at the concept of quality customer service and the impact of the Internet on customer service, it is very essential to note that with the introduction of the Internet in the mid-1990s, the potential for electronic commerce without a doubt, has become a reality-customers shop from a desk at home and surf the Web for interesting home pages to visit. A Website has become the virtual location of pure e-commerce or an alternative channel of distribution for established click-and-mortar retailers (e.g., Barnes & Nobles, Amazon.com, etc,).

In the olden days, the limits of a market were defined by how far a customer would travel to the site, but physical travel is irrelevant in the virtual world of the Internet. Looking at the concept of customer service in the era of technology, it is very important to note that location, however, is still a concern for e-commerce retailers that must ship products and services. This aspect of a business is now driven by access to overnight shippers (e.g., locating a warehouse in Houston for access to FedEx). Internet providers of electronic services, such as brokers, are less reliant on physical offices, and the location of an auction facilitator (e.g., eBay.com) can be based on personal preference of the owners or on access to talented company associates.

As quality customer service and technology (Rust, et al., 2002) take center stage in business operations, it is very important to emphasize that the concept of e-distance, and the barrier it has created and the external navigation, arise from the desire to attract customers to the Website. For example, an undiscovered Website is infinitely distant and one that is five clicks away might rule out 95 percent of the public. Site navigation is a measure of distance, so Website developers often use a two-click rule, i.e., a customer's destination should be no more than two clicks away from the homepage. Locating and getting the Website is another form of distance. If a customer uses a search engine, he/she still needs to read, evaluate, and select a link to follow.

The implications for organizational managers introducing new technology are two-fold. First, what is the overall level of readiness of the customer base affected by the application of new technology-based service? Once this level of readiness is clearly assessed, the extent and appropriate technology to implement, the pace of implementation, and support needed to assist customers will be realized. Second, understanding the technology readiness of company associates is very essential for making the right choices in terms of designing, implementing, and managing the associate interface.

The issue of technology readiness is especially important for contact associates to whom customers may turn for assistance when problems emerge. Company associates who rate high on both interpersonal skills and technology readiness are likely to be good candidates for tech-support roles.

It is very essential to emphasize that as technology continues to evolve, organizations must understand the entire customer journey and creatively apply the right technology at the right time to build greater customer engagement. The Omni-channel approach to customer service provides convenience and accessibility for customers to interact over the channels that they want to use. In reaching this goal, each improvement must not compete with the existing channels. New channels should be introduced at the right level of maturity while early enough to differentiate and deliver the edge over competition. Old channels should be phased-out to keep the operation "lean and mean". Consistent pro-active cross-channel services will put organizations ahead in building and maintaining relationships with their customers.

It is very essential to note that with the concept of customers and services, every event and/or purchase is of some significance for the customer, whereas the same transaction usually is routine for the service producer. Service customers are in most cases motivated to look for a service much as they would for a product;

similarly, their expectations govern their shopping attitudes. Gregory Stone (1954) developed what is now-famous topology in which shopping-goods customers were classified into four groups as follows:

- **The Economizing Customer:** The economizing customer is one who wants to maximize the value obtained for expenditures of time, effort, and money.
- **The Ethical Customer:** The ethical customer is one that feels a moral obligation to patronize socially responsible firms. Service firms that have developed a reputation for community service can create such a loyal customer base; for example, the Ronald McDonald House program for families of hospitalized children has helped the image of McDonald's in this way.
- **The Personalizing Customer:** The personalizing customer is the one who wants interpersonal gratification, such as recognition and conversation, from the service experience. Greeting customers on a first-name basis always has been a staple of the neighborhood family restaurant, but computerized customer files can generate a similar personalized experience when used skillfully by frontline personnel in many other businesses.
- **The Convenience Customer:** The convenience customer is one that has no interest in shopping for the services; convenience is the secret of the attracting factor. It is very important to note that convenience customers often are willing to pay extra for personalized or hassle-free services; for example, supermarkets that provide home delivery may appeal to these customers.

Technology is always making strides towards better customer service, and therefore, higher levels of customer loyalty for companies. When it comes to building customer loyalty (Ami,

Re-engineering Customer Service

Sanghvi, 2018), technology is an important ally to have, as it expands your overall reach and maximizes on your ability to offer assistance. It also makes companies feel more personal and close-to-home for customers, all while showing people how quick and efficient your business is. Consider integrating these bits of technology into your customer service, if you haven't already, and be prepared to be stunned by the levels of customer loyalty that follow. Remember that the best thing about customer loyalty is that there is never any kind of limit to it -- customer loyalty can increase and expand, and, if you play your cards right, it will still continue to grow.

As the trend of competition in the global marketplace continues unabated, the importance of flexibility in meeting or exceeding customer expectations has never been greater. The competition has prompted many companies to empower their contact personnel to exercise more autonomy. Giving company employees more discretion requires a selection process that identifies applicants with the potential for adaptability in their interpersonal behaviors. Communication difficulties with customers can be expected to arise even in the best of circumstances, however. Unrealistic customer expectations and unexpected service failures must be dealt with by the contact personnel as they arise. In order for companies to succeed in this highly competitive and saturated global marketplace, innovation and value-added decisions must clearly be embedded in the process that strives to improve efficiency and increased productivity.

A lot of startup and software companies agree that you can leverage in-product messaging to move new customers through a seamless onboarding process and use email to engage customers who are still stuck on a step.

Dr. Bob L Ssekyanzi, PhD.

The application of technology and management science to the modification of existing systems, organizations, processes, and products in order to make them more effective, efficient, and responsive to the level of customers is an important aspect of meeting and surpassing the needs of customers in a quest to provide quality customer service. Responsiveness is a critical need for organizations in industry and elsewhere. It involves providing products and services of demonstrable value to customers, and thereby to those individuals who have a stake in the success of the organization. Reengineering can be carried out at the level of the organization, at the level of organizational processes, or at the level of the products and services that support an organization's activities. The entity to be reengineered can be systems management, process, product, or some combination. In each case, reengineering involves a basic three-phase systems-engineering life cycle comprising definition, development, and deployment of the entity to be reengineered.

According to Stuart Dorman, (2015) heightened financial and competitive pressures in the global marketplace have brought about varied challenges for customer service organizations – and at the moment the coming years look as though the challenges will persist. Because of this it is imperative that customer service directors maintain a dual focus: actively addressing exciting challenges such as increased volumes of social networking interactions and enormous growth in website access via smartphones, while still continuing to focus on optimizing their operational contact center performance to deliver better service with constrained budgets.

"Organizations also need to think more in terms of a phased approach to their contact center technology deployments, staging their projects and investments so that the benefits from initial projects such as Workforce Management, technology

Re-engineering Customer Service

platform refreshes or Unified Communications roll-outs can be realized," continued Stuart. "This way, organizations can adopt a 'self-funding' discipline to subsequent projects, unlocking new budget from previous operational project savings, and creating a compelling business case for further initiatives such as Voice of the Customer, Video and Virtual Assistant initiatives."

The time for 'dipping your toe' in social media (Rust, Roland and Anthony Zahorik, 1993) has now passed: instead you should be monitoring relevant social media channels, leveraging them as powerful self-service knowledge bases, and moving towards being able to engage customers in real time on key networks such as Facebook and Twitter. Inevitably this will demand equipping agents with the tools and skills necessary to take their customer service skills into the social networking space.

It is very important to note that organizations that are really listening to what their customers are saying are driving today's customer service agenda. The global marketplace looks set to be the place where minor/major organizations really start to embrace the link between offering a high quality customer experience, loyalty and longer-term financial success. By gathering customer insight using the latest real time customer feedback applications, organizations can instantly measure metrics such as Net Promoter Scores, agent performance and Customer Effort Scores to measure how easy they are to do business with. Tying this into quality and performance management process gives companies the opportunity to react to feedback, train staff/associates to replicate the behaviors that customers like the most, and fix those processes that are causing frustration.

Cloud computing can play a key role in helping contact centers to operate more efficiently, and can help organizations in striking the right balance between traditional on premise resilience and the flexibility offered by the latest virtualization and cloud-enabled technologies. As the global marketplace landscape continues to change, challenges/opportunities continue to impact how companies operate and implement the process of customer-service. It is important to mention that reengineering is not process modification—it is change—and the two need to be clearly distinguished up front. Customer focus requires total commitment and support from the top to the front line. In order to be functional and effective, management must allow time for research and data collection. This isn't a quick-fix approach. Much effort must be applied to seek input from users, providers, deliverers, customers and decision makers. Establishing check points in order to discuss progress and periods without progress can in every way be the basis of making progress. Overall, the key is communication throughout the entire process.

Successful reengineering projects in diverse industries and locations demonstrate how companies can expand the dimensions of their reengineering projects. Technology has profoundly changed the business landscape and its impact will continue to grow as long as more businesses continue to adopt technologies that add value to customers' lives. Given its role in determining customer experience and satisfaction, no business owner can underplay the value of technological advancement to businesses and customers. Without happy customers a business's death is inevitable. It is, therefore, for this reason that businesses should invest more resources into new technologies that will help them keep customers happy and satisfied, thereby keeping a competitive edge in the marketplace. Customer needs are a priority that gives a clear vision to any organization. When customers are provided with a better service that matches or surpasses their expectations, this builds exceptional loyalty in them. Take action today. Look for ways that you can use technology to add value to the lives

Re-engineering Customer Service

of your customers and you will be setting up your business for success.

With the competitive global marketplace environment and many other business challenges, it is vital and very necessary to leverage the social channels for a superior customer experience. In developing the 21st Century workforce, it is important to understand that your clients are already using more avenues than ever to reach out to you through the Internet and social media. It may be prudent to consider whether if you can deliver expected customer service experiences that your customers want on these same social media channels, as well as many of these emerging communication technologies? Or, will your customers be disappointed when they cannot find anyone there to help. The conclusion is to acquire the right customer service skills to master these new channels. Social media is about engaging. It's about talking to your customers rather than talking at them. It's about listening to their responses and providing feedback. It's about building relationships and community.

Business process re-engineering is not just a change, but actually it is a dramatic change that calls for dramatic improvements. This is only achieved through overhauling the organization structures, job descriptions, performance management, training and most importantly, the sector of IT i.e. Information Technology. Business process re-engineering (BPR) projects have failed sometimes to meet high expectations. Many unsuccessful BPR attempts are due to the confusion surrounding BPR and how it should be performed. It becomes the process of trial and error.

A business process flow diagram is the most primary representation of a business process **(See diagram below)**. Its main purpose is to simplify complex business processes for better understanding. Usually, these diagrams depict the entire flow of a business process and do not include any problems or exceptions that may occur when the process is in action.

To create an ideal business process flow, you first need to make a list of all the tasks required to complete it.

From your task list, separate the human tasks and system tasks. Human tasks are approval or input-based tasks that require human intervention.

On the contrary, system tasks are those that can be automated and completed independently without any human involvement. These tasks can include calculating data, pulling information from database, sending emails, and copying data from one application to the other.

With all the tasks finalized, you need to decide the sequence in which all the tasks will be executed. Of course, the correct sequence will depend on the business process flow. You can also create alternate or parallel tasks, depending on the data going through the workflow. Each task should also have a deadliness attached to it.

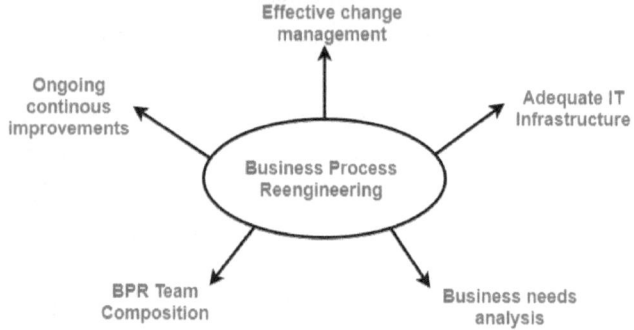

What are the advantages of creating a business process flow?

Better visibility and transparency

With a business process flow, you can better **visualize** how processes are functioning within your organization without any manual monitoring. There is also greater transparency that can give your team members a better understanding of the processes. You can also easily modify the process structure while constantly tracking results.

Higher productivity

When companies take advantage of business process flows, they can determine how a process would function under specific conditions and adjust the process to achieve optimal results. As manual tasks are automated, this action eliminates redundancies and room for error, which in turn improves overall productivity.

Compliance and security

Since each task in a business process is clearly mapped out with detailed workflows, organizations can ensure that all the necessary records and documentation are in place for meeting the required compliance standards. A carefully documented business process also creates a framework for better security.

REFERENCES

Aftab, Alam, (2017) "Amazing Technology" Verit Nation- Tesla's Model 3-Tech Business/Technology June 20, 2017.

Allan, E. Alter, (1990). "The Corporate Make-Over," pp. 32-42.

Brown, Tom J., and Amna Kirmani, (1999). **"The Affluence of Preencounter Affect on Satisfaction with an Anxiety-Provoking Service Encounter."** Journal of Service Research 1, No. 4, pp.333-46.

Champy, James (1995). Re-engineering Management: **The Mandate for New Leadership**. Harper Business.

Dean, A.M., (2007). **"The Impact of the Customer Orientation of Call Center Employees' Affective Commitment and Loyalty."** Journal of Service Research, Vol. 10 No. 2, pp.161-73.

Davenport, Thomas, H., (1993). **Process Innovation: Re-engineering Work Through Information Technology**. Harvard Business School Press.

Hall, Gene, Jim Rosenthal, and Judy Wade. **"How to Make Re-engineering Really Work."** Harvard Business Review, November/December 1993, pp.119-131

Harris, Kim, and Steve Brown, (2004). **"Consumer-to-Consumer Conversation in Service Settings."** Journal of Service Research 6, No. 3, pp. 287-303.

Hill, Terry, (2000). **Manufacturing Strategy**, 3rd ed. New York: Irwin/McGrow-Hill.

Hof, Robert, D., (1999). "A New Era of Bright Hopes and Terrible Fears." Business Week. (October 4) pp. 84-98.

http://www.bls.gov/emp (2004). *U.S. Employment by Industry,*

Ines, Van Gennip, (2018). **"Defining the Customer Experience"** Journal of Research 8, No. 12, pp. 104-107.

"In-Product Messaging" Wikipedia Foundation, 29 July 2016 Wikipedia.org/wiki/"**In-Product _Messaging**"

Miller, Mike, (1994). **"Customer Service Re-engineering"** Personnel Journal, Vol. 73, No. 11, pp. 87-91

Pauline, Ashenden, (2015) http://www.eptica.com/blog/importance-empathy-customer-service-interactions.

Prokesch, Steven, (1995). **"Competing on Customer Service."** Harvard Business Review, pp. 101-12.

Rust, Roland, T., and P.K. Kannan,(2002). (Eds.). **E-Service**. Armonk, New York: M.E. Sharpe.

Rust, Roland T. and Anthony J. Zahorik (1993), **"Customer Satisfaction, Customer Retention, and Market Share,"** Journal of Retailing, No. 69 Vol. 2, pp. 193-215.

Sanghavi, Ami, (2018). **"How to Build Customer Trust and Loyalty through Technology"** The Marketing Zen Group, Vol. 65, No. 10, pp. 1-12.

Stone, Gregory, P., (1954). **"Shoppers and Urban Identification: Observations on the Social Psychology of City Life,"** American Journal of Psychology, pp.36-43

Stuart, Dorman, (2015). **"Customer Service Technology Trends."** Customer Service Managers & Professionals, pp. 6-12.

Tansik, David, A., and William L. Smith, (2000). **"Scripting the Service Encounter."** In New Service Development, eds. J.A. Fitzsimmons and M.J. Fitzsimmons. Thousand Oaks, California: Sage Publications, pp. 239-63.

Werbach, Kevin, (2000). **"Syndication: The Emerging Model for Business in the Internet Era,"** Harvard Business Review, pp. 85-93.

Zeithaml, V.A., Bitner, M.J., (2003). **"Service Marketing: Integrating Customer Focus Across the Firm)**. 3rd ed. McGraw-Hill, New York.

Zetlin, Minda, (2007). "Helping Customers Help Each Other Online". IncTechnology.com

DEDICATION

To my beautiful wife Anna,
Thank you very much for being a source of
happiness, love and support in all ways.
To our children Bob Jr., Penny, Rehema,
and Brenda, and Sebastian,
Thank you very much for being a reflection of
family, and God's love. We love you dearly.
To our grandchildren: Jamila, Ava, Christy,
Sunshine, Siinza and Denzel, we love you so
much and thank God for all the blessings.
To our late parents:
John, Philly and Margaret,
Thank you for everything learned from you.
May your souls rest in peace (RIP)

ABOUT THE AUTHOR

Dr. Ssekyanzi was born and raised in Uganda, East Africa. Attended Nsambya Primary & Junior School, attended St. Bernad's College-Kisweera, St. Henry's College-Kitovu, and on to the University of Nairobi-Kenya. He worked for the Uganda government in various departments as a Senior Accounting Executive for 13 years.

In 1988 he migrated to the United States and joined Sisters of Charity Houston, (SCH) Credit Union as a Treasurer for two years, and in 1990 joined Alcon Research company. an affiliate of Nestle group of companies where he worked in various departments until his retirement in 2014.

Dr. Ssekyanzi has a Bachelor's degree, and a Master's degree from LeTourneau University, Longview, Texas, and a Doctorate degree in Business Administration and International Operations from Jones International University, Centennial, Colorado, United States of America.

Dr. Ssekyanzi is the Founder, owner, & Executive Partner of Braf Business Consultants & Traders (BBCT) a small business consulting company which focuses in providing consultation services in the supply-chain management and other operational services for small start-up companies. Braf Business Consultants & Traders (BBCT) is a **BBB 2024 Winner of Excellence Distinction Award**

Dr. Ssekyanzi is married to his beautiful wife-Anna, with two beautiful daughters, and sons-Bob Jr., and Sebastian, with 6 grandchildren 5 of whom are in Uganda where his son resides with his family, and one is here in the United States.

Dr. Ssekyanzi is the author of the book titled: **The Changing Global Marketplace Landscape.**

www.ingramcontent.com/pod-product-compliance
Lightning Source LLC
Chambersburg PA
CBHW020446220526
45464CB00002B/886